WELCOME

Listener,
Seeker,
Speaker

*A collection of cards, the tarot uses
visual symbolism as a gateway between
the subconscious mind and the conscious one.*

TAROT OF THE DIVINE USES DEITIES, FOLKLORE, FAIRY TALES,
MYTHS, AND LEGENDS FROM AROUND THE WORLD
TO REPRESENT THE DIFFERENT THEMES IN
A TRADITIONAL TAROT DECK.

This deck was created as an homage to the stories we have told one another across cultures and throughout history. While each story is unique to a specific time and place, every culture has stories of bright young adventurers, forbidden doors, or promised lands. In this way, the *Tarot of the Divine* fosters appreciation of our differences and of the truth in our similarities.

A number of these stories will be familiar to Western audiences, but many will be new. Some are short and sweet, while others are pieces of larger epics. This guidebook lists the name of each tale and its country of origin, offering a small window into other cultures. Be sure to check out the accompanying book, *Beneath the Moon*, for a full telling of each story.

HOW TO READ TAROT:

Each card in a tarot deck has a particular meaning, but the reader's intuition is possibly the most valuable part of a reading. While this book provides suggested interpretations for each card, the personal connections you make with the imagery and stories are just as important.

THE MAJOR ARCANA represents what is often called the Fool's journey, with each card representing an archetype or obstacle met on the universal path toward understanding. Cards 1 to 21 represent a hero's odyssey from naïve child to self-actualized adult. Card 0, the Fool, represents the hero themselves. Collectively, these cards are considered powerful, life-focusing cards. Many tarot readers will limit their readings to these 22 cards.

THE MINOR ARCANA is made of 56 cards divided into four suits. These cards represent smaller moments on the Fool's journey. They can best be understood by exploring the intersection of their suit and numerical meanings, found below.

THE SUITS:

CUPS: Spirituality, water, emotions, and feelings

COINS: Materialism, earth, wealth, and physicality

SWORDS: Intellect, air, understanding, and the mind

WANDS: Creativity, fire, vitality, and the heart

THE NUMBERS:

ACE: Beginnings, Inspiration

TWO: Balance, Choices

THREE: Movement, Teetering

FOUR: Stability, Manifestation

FIVE: Power, Conflict

SIX: Harmony, Adjustment

SEVEN: Desire, Reevaluation

EIGHT: Rebirth, Change

NINE: Anticipation, Reflection

TEN: Completion, Renewal

PAGE: The Future

KNIGHT: The Messenger

QUEEN: The Heart

KING: The Ruler

UPRIGHT AND REVERSED MEANINGS:

While each card has a suggested meaning in its upright position, it also has different interpretations when it is upside down. Some readers interpret reversed cards as having the opposite meaning of the upright card, while others attribute unique meanings to each reversed card. Some readers do not use reversed cards at all. Trust your instincts. Assign meaning based on what feels right to you.

SPREADS:

Spreads are suggested card layouts to use for your tarot reading. There is no right or wrong way to lay out a spread—again, let intuition be your guide. What follows are a few common spreads that are especially good for beginners.

Before laying down your cards, lightly shuffle the deck while meditating on a question or opening your mind to intention. Cut the deck and put the top card face down in your chosen spread. Complete the spread by placing cards face down in a particular sequence, and then flip over each card one at a time, in order.

ONE-CARD SPREAD

While not technically a spread, pulling a single card is great for a simple, quick read. This can be used for:

YES-OR-NO QUESTIONS

+ OR +

AS A GENERAL FORECAST FOR THE DAY OR MONTH

THREE-CARD SPREAD

Three-card spreads are versatile and layered. When seeking situational insight, the cards may represent the past, present, and future or the states of your mind, body, and spirit. When faced with a specific choice, three cards may represent option one, option two, and what needs to be considered to choose.

The Moon	 *Queen of Wands*	*Death*
1. OPTION ONE	2. OPTION TWO	3. WHAT NEEDS TO BE CONSIDERED

When experiencing communication difficulties, three cards may represent what you want, what another person may want, and where the conversation is heading.

Feel free to create your own spreads, just be certain your intentions are clear before you pull and place your cards.

Justice	*Ten of Cups*	*The Sun*
1. WHAT ANOTHER PERSON MAY WANT	2. WHAT YOU WANT	3. WHERE THE CONVERSATION IS HEADING

FIVE-CARD SPREAD

In five-card spreads, the cards begin to play off of one another to create new meanings. A spread with many cup cards, for example, may indicate an intensity of emotion. While larger spreads take more time to read, they can offer more insight and guidance. A traditional five-card spread may look something like this:

In this particular spread, the center three cards represent the past, present, and future of the situation in question. The fourth card shows unseen influences affecting the situation. The fifth card represents the potential for an alternate future. If the situation plays out naturally, card 3 is the likely result. If the reader takes card 4 into consideration, however, card 5 is where the path may lead.

A SAMPLE CARD INTERPRETATION:

VI – *The Lovers*
THE BEAUTY AND THE BEAST

An initial reading of this card may suggest love, romance, and connection.

The story of Beauty and the Beast also involves themes of power imbalance, growth, the choice to stay or leave, and, ultimately, a couple learning to complement each other.

To interpret this card, a reader may choose what part of the story resonates most. What speaks to a card reader might change depending on other cards in a spread, the reader's intuition, or their personal connection to the story.

Consider the visual symbolism of the roses. Red roses often represent love, but their thorns make them unapproachable, perhaps alluding to unattainable beauty. Consider the art itself. While Beauty is rendered in watery blues and the Beast in fiery reds, the building in the distance is purple. This could symbolize a compromise, harmony. Or it could be a depiction of The Tower—one of the symbols of the Major Arcana—which represents unexpected destruction.

While this may seem like a lot of information to a new reader, what's most important is to relax and listen to your intuition. Enjoy the experience of connecting with your subconscious and let the cards guide you.

Page of Coins

5. HIDDEN POTENTIAL

Nine of Cups

2. THE PAST

Two of Cups

1. THE PRESENT

Nine of Coins

3. THE CURRENT FUTURE

Nine of Swords

4. UNSEEN INFLUENCES

THE MAJOR ARCANA

The Fool

The Magician

THE LITTLE MERMAID
DENMARK, Danish Fairy Tale

The Fool rests on the pinnacle of a decision. She is ready to dive out of her subconscious and into the physical world. To transform from an animal into a human. She is carefree and excited by a new life, regardless of warnings.

UPRIGHT MEANING: *Beginnings, possibilities, impulsiveness, innocence, a free spirit*

REVERSED MEANING: *Apathy, hesitation, a faulty choice, doldrums, recklessness*

THE FAIRY GODMOTHER
FRANCE, French Fairy Tale

The Magician is a helping hand. She has the ability to change raw materials into something wonderful, and dreaming into doing. But she is only the helping hand; it is up to the protagonist to use her support, moving forward to do the right thing.

UPRIGHT: *Originality, self-confidence, skill, a breakthrough, resourcefulness*

REVERSED: *Insecurity, delay, lack of imagination, closed doors, manipulation*

THE MAJOR ARCANA

The High Priestess

The Empress

SCHEHERAZADE
TURKEY, Arabic Folk Tale

The High Priestess is a keeper of vast knowledge. With a story for every situation, Scheherazade asks the listener to focus on what their subconscious tells them, encouraging them to form their own conclusions. Her power is vast yet subtle, her answers always mysterious.

UPRIGHT: *Wisdom, intuition, dreams, meandering, an enigma*

REVERSED: *Ignorance, shallowness, lack of trust, a closed mind, secrets*

OUR LADY OF GUADALUPE
MEXICO, Catholic Saint

The Empress is a loving and protective mother. She cares for and wishes to defend all of her children, even if a mother's love can sometimes be smothering. The world feels bright, and everything blooms around her.

UPRIGHT: *Fertility, nurturing, accomplishment, nature, abundance*

REVERSED: *Feeling undesirable, anxiety, lack of concentration, smothering, selfishness*

THE MAJOR ARCANA

The Emperor

KING ARTHUR
BRITAIN, Celtic Legend

The Emperor is the ideal father figure. A warrior and a conqueror, King Arthur rules over his kingdom and his sometimes-unruly knights with a just and firm hand. He unifies the fractious, defends the weak, and lends his knowledge and understanding to all his subjects.

UPRIGHT: *Stability, leadership, bravery, bold action, structure*

REVERSED: *Immaturity, pettiness, rigidity, domination, anger*

The Hierophant

WHITE BUFFALO WOMAN
NORTH DAKOTA, Lakota Deity

The Hierophant is a divine figure and teacher who shares the rules, rites, and rituals to follow as a community. There is a place for everyone, and everyone in their place. She encourages the comfort and support of the group, the path well-trodden.

UPRIGHT: *Conformity, compassion, social approval, tradition, legacy*

REVERSED: *Bucking trends, vulnerability, feeling adrift, blind faith*

THE MAJOR ARCANA

The Lovers

The Chariot

THE BEAUTY AND THE BEAST
CHINA, Danish Fairy Tale

The Lovers card represents romance, opposites attracting. The duality and balance of carnality, physicality, and fire versus spirituality, emotions, and water. The pair emphasize the importance of communication and herald an important crossroads.

UPRIGHT: *Love, harmony, trust, a leap of faith, choice*

REVERSED: *Unreliability, separation, second-guessing, values, conflict*

THE THREE PRINCESSES OF WHITELAND
NORWAY, Norwegian Fairy Tale

The Chariot is about harnessing emotions and charging down a straight, clear path. Where the prince may have floundered before, he has learned from his mistakes and now blazes forward confidently.

UPRIGHT: *A journey, perseverance, rushed decisions, vengeance, victory*

REVERSED: *A lack of direction, floundering, stagnation, willfulness*

THE MAJOR ARCANA

Strength

The Hermit

TAM LIN
SCOTLAND, Scottish Fairy Tale

The Strength card is about willpower and determination. Focus, persistence, and the ability to confidently stare any challenge in the face and overcome it. This is not physical strength, but a purity of heart and purpose.

UPRIGHT: *Courage, conviction, control, determination, patience*

REVERSED: *Weakness, self-doubt, abuse of power, pride, negligence*

DRUID AND WHITE STAG
IRELAND, Celtic Legend

The Hermit represents solitude and leaving responsibilities behind to focus inward. In the Celtic myth, the elusive White Stag encourages people to drop everything and pursue spirituality.

UPRIGHT: *Introspection, withdrawal, prudence, insight, meditation*

REVERSED: *Recklessness, hastiness, avoidance, loneliness, rejection*

THE MAJOR ARCANA

The Wheel of Fortune

ANANSI
GHANA, Akan Mythology

The Wheel of Fortune is endlessly turning, spun by a trickster god. What was once luck is now misfortune; what was hopeless is now joyous. These acts may seem random, but all fates are part of an interconnected web of repercussions.

UPRIGHT: *Fortune, an unexpected windfall, karma, destiny, cycles*

REVERSED: *Bad luck, a lack of control, the past, misery, disappointment*

Justice

AMHAENG-EOSA
KOREA, Korean Legend

Justice is power wielded with both intelligence and impartiality. It is making decisions with all of the facts and accepting the consequences of any choice made. It is punishment of the corrupt and promotion of the deserving.

UPRIGHT: *Harmony, balance, equality, virtue, honor*

REVERSED: *Bias, false accusations, intolerance, abuse, dishonesty*

THE MAJOR ARCANA

The Hanged Man

Death

SLEEPING BEAUTY
ITALY, Italian Fairy Tale

The Hanged Man ceases forward momentum to avoid disaster and instead favors reflection. Sleeping Beauty is a symbol of stasis; with the options of sleep or death, she chooses to wait for more favorable conditions.

UPRIGHT: *Suspension, restriction, sacrifice, readjustment, improvement*

REVERSED: *Willfulness, useless sacrifice, rushing, thoughtlessness, martyrdom*

WHITE BEAR KING VALEMON
NORWAY, Norwegian Fairy Tale

Death is a huge upheaval, potentially representing the death of one way of life and the start of a new one. Life changes irrevocably, and there is no way to go back—change is necessary. The death of childhood is important in order to grow up.

UPRIGHT: *Metamorphosis, evolution, loss, transition, change*

REVERSED: *Stagnation, immobility, stubbornness, festering, decay*

Temperance

BODHISATTVA AVALOKITESHVARA
INDIA, Buddhist Bodhisattva

Temperance is about balance and meditation. It is being mutable, recognizing when to change with the times and when to change the situation itself. The Bodhisattva Avalokiteshvara identities are fluid, but their goodwill remains constant.

UPRIGHT: *Moderation, harmony, purpose, good influence, reconciliation*

REVERSED: *Conflict, hostility, frustration, impatience, reluctance*

The Devil

BOITATÁ
BRAZIL, Brazilian Mythology

The Devil gives into the ego, lusting for unnecessary or harmful things, unwilling to leave negative situations. It is a dragon sitting upon a pile of gold it does not need, a person setting a forest on fire for their own gain.

UPRIGHT: *Greed, controversy, violence, strange experiences, addiction*

REVERSED: *Release, enlightenment, power reclaimed, divorce, moving on*

THE MAJOR ARCANA

The Tower — XVI

The Star — XVII

RAPUNZEL
GERMANY, German Fairy Tale

The Tower is about feeling safe and secure before everything is suddenly upended. Beliefs are shattered, understandings ruptured, and everything is destroyed right down to the very foundation. Perhaps the foundation was flawed to begin with.

UPRIGHT: *Massive change, upheaval, catastrophe, rebuilding, revelation*

REVERSED: *Feeling trapped, delaying disaster, fear of pain, avoidance*

SISTER ALYONUSHKA AND BROTHER IVANUSHKA
RUSSIA, Russian Fairy Tale

The Star is a symbol of hope after a disaster. The need to remain positive after misfortune, to remember that things can get better again. It is staying calm and open to future possibilities, seeing your situation with open eyes, mind, and heart.

UPRIGHT: *Hope, serenity, inspiration, insight, spirituality*

REVERSED: *Crushed dreams, insecurity, despair, dejection, exhaustion*

THE MAJOR ARCANA

The Moon

PRINCESS KAGUYA
JAPAN, Japanese Fairy Tale

The Moon is the subconscious and all its illusions, potential, pitfalls, and the possibility of self-deception. Here, two tanukis—shape-shifting raccoon-like animals—each stare at a different moon, though it is not clear which is the real one.

UPRIGHT: *Trickery, melancholy, anguish, illusion, insecurity*

REVERSED: *Joy, enlightenment, resolution, deception revealed, relief*

The Sun

SUN GOD RA
EGYPT, Egyptian Deity

The Sun is success, birth, confidence after passing through difficult times. Egyptian Sun God Ra proves everything is illuminated with optimism and enthusiasm for the path ahead.

UPRIGHT: *Satisfaction, accomplishment, joy, luck, vitality*

REVERSED: *Missed opportunities, delays, doubt, fear of missing out, depression*

THE MAJOR ARCANA

Judgment

The World

SUN WUKONG, THE MONKEY KING
CHINA, Chinese Mythology

Judgment is the reckoning, an ending before the start of a new journey. Past actions and decisions determine future events. If you haven't learned your lessons, you are doomed to repeat your mistakes over and over.

UPRIGHT: *Improvement, forgiveness, a change of perspective, absolution, rebirth*

REVERSED: *Oppression, lack of self-awareness, failure, repeated mistakes, self-loathing*

HINEMOA AND TUTANEKAI
NEW ZEALAND, Maori Legend

The World is the happily-ever-after ending following a difficult journey. Hinemoa and Tutanekai represent the victorious conclusion, a positive outcome most desired. However, a conclusion also heralds the start of a new journey.

UPRIGHT: *Completion, recognition, fulfillment, triumph, celebration*

REVERSED: *Imperfection, disappointment, shortcuts, shortsightedness, anxiety*

THE MINOR ARCANA: CUPS

Ace of Cups

Two of Cups

MATSUO'S SAKE
JAPAN, Japanese Mythology

The Ace of Cups marks a new beginning—a reason to drink and be merry, and to open up to subconscious feelings. Sake is a drink of the gods, bringing people closer to the spirit world.

UPRIGHT: *Happiness, love, intimacy, new emotions, compassion*

REVERSED: *Relationship problems, depression, sadness, creative block, repression*

ENKIDU AND GILGAMESH
IRAQ, Sumerian Mythology

The Two of Cups is an ideal relationship that still faces difficulties. Gilgamesh was a tyrant until Enkidu was created for him—to be his equal in every way. Though their initial meeting was rocky, they came to love each other very much as opposites who complete each other.

UPRIGHT: *A happy relationship, equality, partnership, attraction, connection*

REVERSED: *Imbalance, discord, separation, incompatibility, power imbalance*

THE MINOR ARCANA: CUPS

Three of Cups

Four of Cups

APSARA

CAMBODIA, Hindu Mythology

The Three of Cups represents camaraderie and a good time. The Apsara are celestial beings of the sky known for dancing, partying, and fornication. The joyous group oversees fertility rites, the performing arts, and the fortunes of gambling.

UPRIGHT: *Celebrations, friends, indulgence, parties, community*

REVERSED: *Overindulgence, infidelity, disintegrating bonds, gossip, isolation*

THE NIGHTINGALE

DENMARK, Danish Folk Tale

The Four of Cups represents romanticizing bad choices while ignoring the good alternatives before you. It is coveting what is superficially "better," neglecting a plain nightingale who can actually sing away death.

UPRIGHT: *A lack of awareness, pessimism, daydreaming, lethargy, reevaluation*

REVERSED: *Motivation, opportunity, optimism, restlessness, boredom*

Five of Cups

Six of Cups

LA LLORONA
MEXICO, Mexican Folklore

The Five of Cups is useless regret without learning. Jealous of her husband's new wife, La Llorona drowns her own children and now her wailing ghost wanders the earth. She continues to wallow in grief, refusing to seek redemption or happiness.

UPRIGHT: *Self-pity, guilt, regret, stagnation, depression*

REVERSED: *Moving on, forgiveness, acceptance, finding peace, encouragement*

THE SNOW QUEEN
DENMARK, Danish Fairy Tale

The Six of Cups evokes a nostalgia for sweeter times. Kai and Gerda are best friends as children, but when Kai is struck with depression, he leaves with the Snow Queen. Through many adventures, Gerda saves him, but by then, innocence is gone.

UPRIGHT: *Nostalgia, old friends, simple joys, sharing, childhood*

REVERSED: *The future, letting go, leaving home, rose-tinted glasses*

THE MINOR ARCANA: CUPS

Seven of Cups

Eight of Cups

ALADDIN
PERSIA, Arabic Folk Tale

The Seven of Cups shows Aladdin standing before a myriad of fantastical dreams. It is impossible for him to pursue them all, and it is important he makes his decision wisely and quickly.

UPRIGHT: *Daydreaming, fantasy, decisions, wishful thinking, procrastination*

REVERSED: *Reality, clarity, temptation, confusion, diversion*

MOSES
EGYPT, Hebrew Legend

The Eight of Cups represents leaving good things behind in the pursuit of higher ideals. Moses was raised as a prince of Egypt, but realized he needed to sacrifice his royal life and wealth to pursue a spiritual and ascetic one.

UPRIGHT: *Walking away, introspection, escapism, withdrawal, seeking truth*

REVERSED: *Aimlessness, fear of abandonment, depression, settling, hopelessness*

THE MINOR ARCANA: CUPS

Nine of Cups

Ten of Cups

TÀJ AL-MULÚK AND THE PRINCESS DUNYÀ
IRAN, Arabic Folk Tale

The Nine of Cups represents a happy ending achieved in unexpected ways. Prince Tāj al-Mulúk fell in love with Princess Dunyà, but she refused men. He used trickery, disguising himself as a woman in order to win her heart.

UPRIGHT: *Dreams realized, fulfillment, pleasure, recognition, triumph*

REVERSED: *Greed, devastation, pessimism, addiction, self-loathing*

JULNAR THE SEA-BORN
PERSIA, Arabic Folk Tale

The Ten of Cups represents true emotional and spiritual fulfilment. After many hard trials, Julnar finds a happy, loving husband and has a child. Her brother rises from the sea, which often represents the subconscious, to congratulate her and celebrate her newfound life.

UPRIGHT: *Harmony, reunions, security, domestic bliss, found family*

REVERSED: *Dysfunctional family, broken home, instability, conflict, neglect*

THE MINOR ARCANA: CUPS

Page of Cups

Knight of Cups

BAKUNAWA AND THE SEVEN MOONS
PHILIPPINES, Filipino Mythology

The Page of Cups is connected to his emotions and expresses himself wholly with youthful purity. In this card, one of the seven young moon siblings plays with Tu'er Shen, the Chinese god of same-sex relationships who ties the red thread of fate that connects lovers.

UPRIGHT: *Youthfulness, idealism, sensitivity, romance, spirituality*

REVERSED: *Bad news, jealousy, obsession, childhood problems, immaturity*

HALIBU THE HUNTER
MONGOLIA, Mongolian Legend

The Knight of Cups is a messenger. Halibu is kind and gentle while also willing to take a stand for what he believes in. Halibu provides for his village, and after befriending a dragon, he willingly sacrifices himself to save everyone he loves.

UPRIGHT: *Chivalry, affection, invitations, taking action, meaningful gifts*

REVERSED: *Heartbreak, infidelity, lack of diplomacy, moodiness, pettiness*

THE MINOR ARCANA: CUPS

Queen of Cups

King of Cups

YEMOJA
NIGERIA, Yoruba Deity

The Queen of Cups represents the surface of the subconscious. The goddess Yemoja connects those on land to the depth of the spiritual plane. She is mysterious but also a kind and caring mother.

UPRIGHT: *Femininity, warmth, empathy, a counselor, intuition*

REVERSED: *Immaturity, selfishness, smothering, sulking, spite*

THE BOY AND THE DRAGON PEARL
CHINA, Chinese Legend

The King of Cups was once a little boy but has matured into a powerful dragon. He is kind but fiercely protective of those he loves. He is connected to the deep dark waters of the subconscious. He possesses great patience and wisdom.

UPRIGHT: *Devotion, loyalty, faithfulness, wisdom, generosity*

REVERSED: *Anxiety, lack of caring, control, violence, imbalance*

THE MINOR ARCANA: COINS

Ace of Coins

Two of Coins

JACK AND THE BEANSTALK
ENGLAND, English Fairy Tale

The Ace of Coins presents us with new beginnings, financial opportunities, and prosperity. The origin of this gift may be unexpected—like magical beans—but through nourishment and support, the benefits could be miraculous. It's time to make dreams a reality.

UPRIGHT: *New business, money, investments, abundance, security*

REVERSED: *Bad finances, excessive spending, greed, stinginess, poor planning*

RHPISUNT
PACIFIC NORTHWEST, Haida Mythology

The Two of Coins represents the skill needed to balance opposing forces in life. For Rhpisunt, the bear world and the human world collide. She embodies the dualities of work and family, hobbies and careers, and wants versus needs.

UPRIGHT: *Multitasking, balance, choice, flexibility, prioritization*

REVERSED: *Disorganization, a façade, overwhelm, overextending, financial mess*

THE MINOR ARCANA: COINS

Three of Coins

Four of Coins

BANJHAKRI AND BANJHAKRINI
NEPAL, Tamang Mythology

The Three of Coins represents learning from one another. The fierce Banjhakri and Banjhakrini teach their apprentice how to become a shaman. They are demanding teachers, but their student is dedicated. All three put in hard work that pays off with the success of a new generation.

UPRIGHT: *Studying, growth, collaboration, success, recognition*

REVERSED: *Poor work ethic, apathy, lack of goals, willfulness*

CONDOR'S WIFE
PERU, Aymara Folk Tale

The Four of Coins represents greed and an unwillingness to open up or share. Condor covets his wife, who does not like his lifestyle or living with him. He recognizes her unhappiness but is unwilling to make changes or set her free.

UPRIGHT: *Hoarding, possession, financial stability, materialism, stinginess*

REVERSED: *Gambling, recklessness, letting go, generosity, large purchases*

THE MINOR ARCANA: COINS

Five of Coins

Six of Coins

THE LITTLE MATCH GIRL
DENMARK, Danish Fairy Tale

The Five of Coins represents financial hardship and feeling left in the cold. The Little Match Girl needs help, but no one is willing to help her. She struggles alone, despite her proximity to a force that could potentially help her.

UPRIGHT: *Recession, adversity, isolation, unemployment, ruin*

REVERSED: *Paid debts, improved finances, positive change, acceptance, recovery*

THE WOMAN WHO WAS KIND TO INSECTS
ALASKA, Inuit Fable

The Six of Coins represents kindness and generosity to those less fortunate. The old woman from this Inuit tale understands the need to put positivity into the world in order to receive it back—the pay-it-forward methodology of karma.

UPRIGHT: *Generosity, charity, kindness, value, reward*

REVERSED: *Abuse of power, scams, extortion, gullibility, greed*

THE MINOR ARCANA: COINS

Seven of Coins

Eight of Coins

NANAHUATZIN
MEXICO, Aztec Mythology

The Seven of Coins represents the desire for a good harvest, though it might require sacrifice. Nanahuatzin must determine when it is right to be patient and when it is better to scrap everything to start fresh.

UPRIGHT: *Reward, perseverance, decisions, investment, fruition*

REVERSED: *Shortsightedness, laziness, procrastination, setbacks, delay*

SIX SWANS
GERMANY, German Fairy Tale

The Eight of Coins represents the long haul, the slough in the middle of a project that needs to be completed. The little princess needs to keep weaving nettles in silence if she wishes to set her cursed brothers free.

UPRIGHT: *Craftsmanship, commitment, determination, ambition, concentration*

REVERSED: *Repetition, poor quality, rushing, bad reputation*

THE MINOR ARCANA: COINS

Nine of Coins

Ten of Coins

THE LEGEND OF THE WATERMELON
VIETNAM, Vietnamese Legend

The Nine of Coins represents success. Hard work and patience have resulted in a successful harvest, and now, even the Emperor enjoys Mai An Tiêm's watermelons. The road was long and hard, but the rewards well worth the effort.

UPRIGHT: *Independence, prosperity, freedom, maturity, self-discipline*

REVERSED: *Scams, superficiality, overinvestment, work-obsessed, ungrateful*

PAN HU
CHINA, Yao Legend

The Ten of Coins represents the hard-earned rewards of a difficult venture. The story of Pan Hu celebrates the lineage that benefits from his hard work. The hardships he once endured allow him to appreciate his good fortune and retire surrounded by his progeny.

UPRIGHT: *Inheritance, ancestry, pensions, settling down, financial stability*

REVERSED: *Financial disaster, disputes, instability, broken traditions*

THE MINOR ARCANA: COINS

Page of Coins

Knight of Coins

BEAIVI-NIEIDA
SWEDEN, Sami Deity

The Page of Coins welcomes the beginning of spring and summer, a fresh start, the end of darkness. Beaivi-nieida represents hope, setting up solid foundations, and mental wellness. She is grounded and anticipates the bright future.

UPRIGHT: *Setting goals, loyalty, positivity, opportunities, manifestation*

REVERSED: *A lack of common sense, immaturity, laziness, apathy*

HEITSI-EIBIB
SOUTH AFRICA, Khoikhoi Deity

The Knight of Coins is a diligent warrior who is willing to put in the work to set the world right. Heitsi-Eibib can be as stubborn as an ox, getting into trouble for his efforts. He is strong, loyal, and determined in all things he sets his mind to.

UPRIGHT: *Ambition, hard work, persistence, being efficient*

REVERSED: *Impatience, apathy, irresponsibility, anxiety*

THE MINOR ARCANA: COINS

Queen of Coins

King of Coins

WARAMURUNGUNDJU
NORTHERN AUSTRALIA, Gunwinggu Deity

The Queen of Coins is an eager mother, ready to bring new life. Waramurungundju has traveled the world blessing her many children. She is always moving; loving and ever-practical, she teaches her children how to help themselves.

UPRIGHT: *A healer, luxury, being grounded, practicality, movement*

REVERSED: *Jealousy, possession, a lack of organization, manipulation*

HAH-NU-NAH, THE WORLD TURTLE
NORTH AMERICA, Iroquois Mythology

The King of Coins represents stability and faithfulness. The World Turtle is strong enough to support the weight of others' hopes and dreams. He may not be an active participant in their lives, but he is always dependable, slow, and steady.

UPRIGHT: *Success, dependability, conservatism, strong will, willing to work*

REVERSED: *Corruption, materialism, ruthlessness, authority, indulgence*

THE MINOR ARCANA: SWORDS

Ace of Swords

Two of Swords

GORDIAN KNOT
TURKEY, Greek Legend

The Ace of Swords represents a sudden burst of inspiration. A new solution, a new way of thinking to break through a problem. Slicing through the Gordian Knot begins a campaign to conquer new lands.

UPRIGHT: *New projects, truth, assertiveness, creative thinking, clarity*

REVERSED: *Lack of communication, misinformation, rigidity, confusion*

SITA
INDIA, Hindu Epic Ramayana

The Two of Swords represents being stuck between hard choices. Sita's decision between Scylla and Charybdis is not easy and cannot be made blindly; it calls for self-reflection. Things can only remain balanced for so long before a move must be made.

UPRIGHT: *Facing fears, a stalemate, denial, opposition, a precarious position*

REVERSED: *Indecision, lies exposed, delays, overwhelming fear*

THE MINOR ARCANA: SWORDS

Three of Swords

Four of Swords

CRANE WIFE
JAPAN, Japanese Fairy Tale

The Three of Swords represents betrayal. The Crane Wife asks her husband for privacy, but he spies on her, only to discover she was hurting herself to help him. His spying was treacherous, but so was her inability to trust him with her secret.

UPRIGHT: *Heartbreak, self-harm, sadness, grief, separation*

REVERSED: *Overcoming grief, optimism, reconciliation, forgiveness, seeking help*

FENRIR
NORWAY, Norse Mythology

The Four of Swords signals a pause in battle. The Norse gods know that the wolf, Fenrir, will bring about the end of the world, so they have him bound and chained. While he still represents a threat, for now there is respite.

UPRIGHT: *Sanctuary, recouping, meditation, passivity, counseling*

REVERSED: *Awakening, healing, returning, burnout, strength*

THE MINOR ARCANA: SWORDS

Five of Swords

Six of Swords

OSIRIS, SET, AND ISIS
EGYPT, Egyptian Mythology

The Five of Swords represents a fight won through deceit. Set overthrows his brother Osiris and is seen gloating over his brother's inconsolable wife, Isis. While Set represents a tyrant of a victor, Isis is a defeated combatant who will eventually bring about Set's defeat.

UPRIGHT: *Surrender, betrayal, bullying, violence, crime*

REVERSED: *Resolution, compromise, sacrifice, peace, justice*

DANAË AND PERSEUS
GREECE, Greek Mythology

The Six of Swords represents leaving behind tumultuous waters for a future that is calm and promising. After being imprisoned by her own father, Danaë and her young son Perseus escape. Perseus will eventually grow to defeat the gorgon Medusa.

UPRIGHT: *Healing, moving forward, stability, escape, journeys*

REVERSED: *Feeling trapped, instability, canceled travel, abuse, unresolved issues*

THE MINOR ARCANA: SWORDS

Seven of Swords

Eight of Swords

COYOTE
PACIFIC NORTHWEST, Salish Legend

The Seven of Swords is a trickster, and the coyote represents deceit in all forms—from small pranks to terrible scandals. He is clever and manipulative, but more often than not, he is caught by his own schemes and has to pay dearly for them.

UPRIGHT: *Strategy, cunning, thievery, cheating, manipulation*

REVERSED: *Conscience, confession, getting caught, outsmarted, deception*

DONKEYSKIN
FRANCE, French Fairy Tale

The Eight of Swords represents being caught in up in your own insecurities. Donkeyskin was forced into hiding to escape a bad situation. Now she is faced with the decision to continue the life she has created or to step out of her self-made prison.

UPRIGHT: *Anxiety, victimhood, feeling trapped, paralysis, crisis*

REVERSED: *Freedom, new perspectives, taking a stand, strength, healing*

THE MINOR ARCANA: SWORDS

Nine of Swords

Ten of Swords

OEDIPUS
GREECE, Greek Mythology

The Nine of Swords represents decision-making controlled by anxiety. The Oracle at Delphi warns the king that his son, Oedipus, will one day kill him. Had he not let his fears control him and raised his son in love instead of hate, the king's eventual death could have been avoided.

UPRIGHT: *Anxiety, terror, nightmares, obsession, insomnia*

REVERSED: *Recovery, acceptance, letting go, accepting help, hope*

SEDNA
CANADA, Inuit Mythology

The Ten of Swords represents backstabbing and betrayal. Sedna's father pushes her from his kayak and chops off her fingers when she tries to cling to his boat. She sinks to the bottom of the ocean and becomes consumed with wrath, eternally seeking revenge.

UPRIGHT: *Bitterness, betrayal, rock bottom, martyrdom, severing ties*

REVERSED: *Surviving disaster, recovery, regeneration, the inevitable*

THE MINOR ARCANA: SWORDS

Page of Swords

Knight of Swords

PRINCESS PARIZADE
ANATOLIA, Arabic Folk Tale

The Page of Swords represents youthful intelligence. Princess Parizade uses her wit to succeed where others have failed, her optimism intact through it all. She is a harbinger of new beginnings and new ideas for herself and those around her.

UPRIGHT: *Talkativeness, energy, thoughtfulness, curiosity, truthfulness*

REVERSED: *Bluntness, cynicism, defensiveness, sullenness, all talk*

HANG TUAH
MALAYSIA, Malaysian Legend

The Knight of Swords is a strong and assertive warrior. Hang Tuah—an intelligent soldier—is unafraid of leaping into battle and employing unconventional techniques to win. He is rebellious, loyal, and a fierce champion.

UPRIGHT: *Intellect, bravery, confidence, being action-oriented*

REVERSED: *Rudeness, bullying, an inferiority complex, passivity*

THE MINOR ARCANA: SWORDS

Queen of Swords

King of Swords

TURANDOT
CHINA, Arabic Folk Tale

The Queen of Swords is a fierce and exacting force. Turandot does not forget betrayal, so her judgments, while fair and principled, seem brutal and cold. Still, she is open-minded and intelligent, and can be charming and witty when she chooses.

UPRIGHT: *Protection, meaningful criticism, tough love, skepticism, intelligence*

REVERSED: *Bitterness, vindication, judgment, malice, pessimism*

GRIFFIN
PERSIA, Persian Mythology

The King of Swords represents wisdom enhanced by power. The griffin is a noble and intelligent creature, soaring over land and sea, a symbol for patience, perseverance, and judgment.

UPRIGHT: *Authority, structure, logic, self-discipline, loyalty*

REVERSED: *A dictator, cruelty, violence, oppression, cynicism*

THE MINOR ARCANA: WANDS

Ace of Wands

Two of Wands

THE MAGIC PAINTBRUSH
CHINA, Chinese Folk Tale

The Ace of Wands represents inspiration, a sudden creative force. The magic paintbrush embodies these qualities with passion and daring. The magical moment right before the ink hits the paper and all dreams and possibilities are within reach.

UPRIGHT: *Excitement, creativity, a spark, growth, new beginnings*

REVERSED: *Delays, bad news, a creative block, wasted talent*

JANUS
ITALY, Roman Mythology

The Two of Wands represents travel and commerce. Janus, the god of doorways and transition, is able to look to the past and the future in order to make effective decisions. He is always in motion, connecting dreams with actual possibilities.

UPRIGHT: *Decisions, travel, business opportunities, future planning, cooperation*

REVERSED: *Indecision, doubt, fear of the unknown, playing it safe*

THE MINOR ARCANA: WANDS

Three of Wands

Four of Wands

THE ENCHANTED PIG
ROMANIA, Romanian Fairy Tale

The Three of Wands represents hard work and travel. The princess takes a long journey to rescue her prince, making sacrifices and surviving trials along the way. If she stays motivated, her efforts will be rewarded.

UPRIGHT: *Self-motivation, freedom, reward, romance*

REVERSED: *Returning home, wallowing, frustration, delays*

MOHINI AND ARAVAN
INDIA, Sanskrit Epic Poem

The Four of Wands represents rejoicing and festivities. A well-deserved celebration and a stable time to be thankful, cherishing loved ones. Mohini and Aravan embrace each other, enjoying the time before the next adventure begins.

UPRIGHT: *Reunion, success, pride, happiness, family*

REVERSED: *Self-doubt, diaspora, canceled plans, gloom*

THE MINOR ARCANA: WANDS

Five of Wands

Six of Wands

THE PANDAVAS
INDIA, Sanskrit Epic Poem

The Five of Wands is represented here by The Pandavas—five brothers who embody unity in the face of conflict. The five brothers have been known to bicker and play-fight, but they also care deeply for one another. A resolution to their strife only comes from good communication.

UPRIGHT: *Rivalry, opponents, disagreement, competition, clashing egos*

REVERSED: *Compromise, peace, harmony, resolution, conflict avoidance*

YENNENGA
BURKINA FASO, Mossi Legend

The Six of Wands represents victory and success. A warrior princess, Yennenga is her father's most prized fighter. Her skill is so great he never wishes to part with her, but she rebels. She seeks her own path and recognition for her deeds.

UPRIGHT: *Victory, praise, achievement, reward, fame*

REVERSED: *Ego, pride, disrepute, a fall from grace*

THE MINOR ARCANA: WANDS

Seven of Wands

Eight of Wands

JOHN HENRY
ALABAMA, American Folk Tale

The Seven of Wands represents an indomitable force. Against all odds, John Henry stands up for what he believes in and is willing to fight to the bitter end. His courage and resolve is an inspiration, even to those who disagree with him.

UPRIGHT: *Endurance, attack, fighting for beliefs, perseverance, mounting a defense*

REVERSED: *Giving up, defeat, timidity, cowardice, overwhelmed*

RAINBOW CROW
NORTH AMERICA,
Lenape Legend (Disputed)

The Eight of Wands represents quick, decisive actions. The rainbow crow flies quickly to deliver warmth to the cold earth below, singeing his wings in the process. His sacrifice and swift journey are fruitful.

UPRIGHT: *Speed, momentum, travel, excitement, results*

REVERSED: *Lethargy, delays, bad timing, slowness, frustration*

THE MINOR ARCANA: WANDS

Nine of Wands

Ten of Wands

VASILISA THE BEAUTIFUL
RUSSIA, Russian Fairy Tale

The Nine of Wands represents weathering the battle. Sent by her wicked stepmother to the door of the witch Baba Yaga, Vasilisa the Beautiful stays resilient. She endures Baba Yaga's impossible trials. She is wary and cautious, but also hopeful.

UPRIGHT: *Fatigue, persistence, gathering strength, wounds, resilience*

REVERSED: *A stalemate, stubbornness, hesitance, giving in, paranoia*

TIMBO TREE
PARAGUAY, Guarani Legend

The Ten of Wands represents taking on too much and refusing to accept help. When Saguaa's daughter went missing, he searched alone, in vain. A Timbo tree grew from his ear when he died, bearing fruits he labored for but was unable to enjoy.

UPRIGHT: *Overwhelm, stress, obligation, refusing aide, duty*

REVERSED: *Avoidance, burnout, overcommitting, stretched thin, giving up*

THE MINOR ARCANA: WANDS

Page of Wands

Knight of Wands

MWINDO
REPUBLIC OF THE CONGO, Nyanga Mythology

The Page of Wands represents a childlike optimism and carefree rebellion. For Mwindo, every situation is made fun by a swish of his magical flyswatter. He makes many enemies, but just as many friends who help him in his journey.

UPRIGHT: *Playfulness, charisma, discovery, a rogue, enthusiasm*

REVERSED: *Naïvety, petulance, a lack of imagination, pessimism*

TATTERHOOD
NORWAY, Norwegian Fairy Tale

The Knight of Wands represents a fearless fighter, eager to charge into battle, especially if it means defending someone she loves. Reckless and unafraid, Tatterhood grabs what she wants to claim the future she desires.

UPRIGHT: *Adventure, passion, a rebel, a flirt, a hot temper*

REVERSED: *Arrogance, jealousy, abuse, recklessness, a braggart*

THE MINOR ARCANA: WANDS

Queen of Wands

King of Wands

PELE
HAWAII, Hawaiian Deity

The Queen of Wands represents a fiery force. The volcano goddess Pele's rages can be destructive, but her blessings are just as powerful. She is the creativity of dance the nourishment of rich soil, and the chaotic force of an explosion.

UPRIGHT: *Optimism, independence, confidence, passion, verve*

REVERSED: *Jealousy, spite, avarice, destruction, demands*

THE PHOENIX
EAST ASIA, East Asian Mythology

The King of Wands is a symbol of strength. The legend of the phoenix spans many cultures, but in all of them, the firebird represents nobility, rebirth, strength, and loyalty.

UPRIGHT: *Honesty, passion, leadership, charm, flexibility*

REVERSED: *Tyranny, a lack of harmony, weakness, volatility*

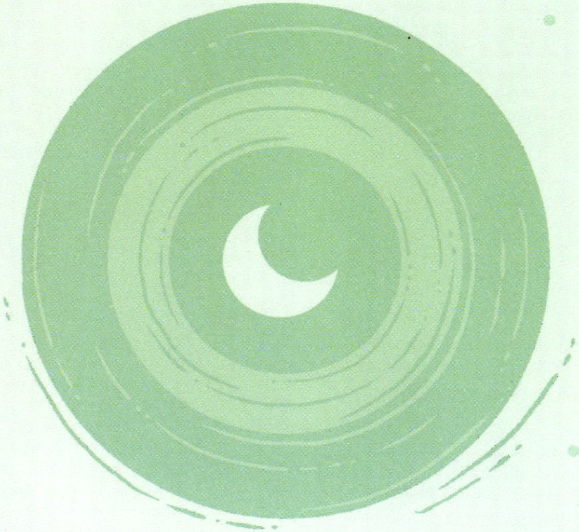

Copyright © 2020 by Yoshi Yoshitani

All rights reserved.

Published in the United States
by Clarkson Potter/Publishers,
an imprint of Random House,
a division of Penguin Random House LLC,
New York.

clarksonpotter.com

CLARKSON POTTER is a trademark and POTTER with colophon is a registered trademark of Penguin Random House LLC.

ISBN 978-0-593-13514-3

Printed in China

Design by Lise Sukhu

Illustrations by Yoshi Yoshitani

16

First Edition